About Franki Ellio

At times mundane, awkward, offensive and ulti-mately, heartbreaking.
- The Paris Review

"Franki's stories have soul and wit but are also made of real flesh and blood."
- Drew Dernavich, cartoonist for *The New Yorker*

Sometimes I run across a poem that makes me sec-ond guess my opinion on poetry. It could be a line in the poem that impresses me. Or a person in the poem that makes me wonder what he'd be like in another situation. Or a relationship that makes me wonder how it worked out. For me...Franki Elliot had all of the above."
- The Chicago Tribune

The poems, stories or prose poems- pick your term-fluctuate from sandpaper interactions between fami-ly members or lovers to dreamlike sequences in which linear narrative disappears."
-Time Out Magazine

Published by Mixed Loves Imprint

Los Angeles, CA, 2018

Second Limited Edition

Copyright © 2018 by Franki Elliot

Library of Congress Control Number: 978069299468 ISBN

Cover art by Shawn Stucky (© 2018)

Cover design Maria Cardenas

Manufactured in the United States of America

stories for people who hate love…

(and other electrical activities of the heart)

by *franki elliot

this book is dedicated to every
person who never texted me back.

(and a special thanks to Shawn Stucky)

Table Of Contents

Palm Reader

I paid a palm reader in East Village
$5.00 and all she said was:

you will love & be loved
but never at the same time.

I wish I had bought a coffee instead.

Smug

I pull on my shirt and say,
a little too smug,

"You always come back to me
when you break up with your girlfriend."

He pulls on his shirt
and says, a little too smug,

"I didn't break up with my girlfriend."

Kintsugi

I mention I have a little collection of him:

- 2 ginger beers in the back of my fridge
- 4 symphony ticket stubs
- a handmade postcard sent from China
- a broken vase he promised to reseal with gold
  (*it's more beautiful for having been broken*)
- a v-neck shirt I hate to admit I still sleep in

- a plastic crown from New Year's Eve

- an unused magnum condom

What does he have of me?

- a small rose quartz crystal that fell out of my pocket
  (*and he tried to give back*)
- the best sex he's ever had
- a copy of my book he'll never read

I Hate Salad

I was at a restaurant eating salad (I never eat salad)
and the girl next to me was eating salad too.

We were minding our own business when an
awkward man came up to her and stammered:

"Excuse me but I think you are
incredibly beautiful."

She nodded, thanked him and they shared
pleasantries until he walked away, empty handed.

I turned to her and said, "That was very brave of
him, coming up to you like that," and she nodded
again.

She said she has a speech prepared to let men off
easy when they approach her with compliments.

She said it as if being desired were a full time job
and the pay was never enough.

We went back to eating our salads and I tried to
imagine what it must feel like to be so universally
beautiful.

Lake Michigan

It was 4AM in Chicago when you led me
to your favorite bench along the lake.

There were spiders and policemen and bums to
dodge but the moonlight dissolved into the water
quite effortlessly.

I pulled out my earbuds, one for you and one for me,
and played a scratchy old recording of
"House of the Rising Sun."

We sat on your favorite bench listening and staring
at the dark water and I told myself to remember this
moment, to carefully tuck it away, in case I needed it.

You reached for your pen and notepad
and began to write a poem,

saying all this
reminded you
of
a girl
you once knew.

And just like that,
the moment
no longer belonged
to me.

The Moon

It's midnight when a disheveled woman
stops me on Hollywood Blvd. and says,

"There's a full moon tonight and I can't find it.
I'm going to call the police and ask them where it is."

I look up and there it is, unmistakable, as always.

I point and her head of white hair turns
toward the sky. She shakes with relief.

"There you are, you tricky motherfucker,"
she says to the moon.

The moon does not respond.

As I walk away I realize I may not have found love
in the corner booth with the shy law student,

and I may not know why cactus flowers
only bloom at night,

and I may not have the answers to the
many things that leave me empty

but tonight I found the moon for a stranger
and it was rich with the milk of human
kindness.

Selfish

He mailed me a note
that simply said: I love you

(because that's the kind of guy he was)

and it arrived three days after
I broke up with him on the phone
for being boring

(because that's the kind of girl I was).

It was the first and last time
he said it

and now I keep searching for the word
that describes wanting someone when
you can no longer have them.

I think the word is selfish.
The word is probably selfish.

The Heart #1

He was distraught when he admitted
his doctor had put him on meds.

"I took them for a week and
then the strangest thing happened,

I was staring at my bedroom ceiling
and realized I could grab the very top
corner and pull the whole world down on me.

That's when I started reading about the side effects."

He reached into his bag for the familiar orange
prescription bottle and shook it.

"Do you know what the tenth most common side
effect of Prozac is?"

I threw some guesses.

"Low key happiness. Not giving a fuck.

The ability to stand in line at the grocery store like a
normal human being."

He pointed to the label and read out loud:
"Changes in the electrical activity of your heart."

I let that sink in.

Changes in the electrical activity
of your heart.

How medical, how sterile,
how borderline poetic.

"That's not a side effect of a pill," I said,

"That's a side effect of life."

Heart #2

I read somewhere that the only organ ancient
Egyptians leave in the body during the embalming
process is the heart.

I also read that a man's heart weighs more than a
woman's, the difference somewhere between
eight and ten ounces

and
some days
my heart is so heavy

it could anchor me
to the bottom of the ocean

like a shipwreck
someone may never discover.

The Heart #3

We were standing in his pristine kitchen
when he asked me if I had ever held
a hummingbird.

"It's like cupping your hands around a tiny,
beating heart and trying desperately not
to let go."

I imagined the restless bird in his palms
and then imagined my restless heart in
them instead

and wondered which
he'd be more careful with.

The Heart #4

There are certain people
I truly believe

should be in love with me
but they aren't.

The Heart #5

Reach into your
blue jeans pocket

and
give
me
back
my heart.

The Heart #6

and
I will never understand
why we disregard the people
who want to love us

while chasing the people
who don't.

The Heart #7

I wanted to give you
back all your things

but then I realized
I didn't have any.

Recipe for fearlessness:

Let go of your mother.
Let go of your father.
Let go of your sister.
Let go of your brother.

Let go of your lover.
Let go of yourself.

Start over.

Te Quiero

Every time I'm in San Francisco
I end up kissing a different Peruvian boy

and they always tell me the English language is
flawed because we have no translation for

the feeling that falls
between "like" and "love"

or maybe it's the feeling
between "lust" and "love"

(te quiero).

As an American, the meaning of this escapes me,
but I want to assume it means "to almost love"

and I hate to admit it but
I'm always almost in love.

Pajama Pants

We are waiting for an elevator at the nursing home
when my mother's wife starts whispering,
"no no no no."

I follow the fear in her eyes and see a stretcher
covered in a white sheet.

The sheet has a gold cross embroidered across it
and a Deacon is standing solemnly to the side.

Suddenly I realize what's about to happen.
We are about to get in the elevator with a dead body.

I lock eyes with The Deacon.
He's maybe sixty, has a mustache and glasses.

I recognize him:
he buried my grandmother ten days earlier.

Ten days ago, my grandfather wore a suit jacket
and pajama pants and sat next to her casket,
looking small and heartbroken in his wheelchair.

When I kissed his cheek, he simply said:
I don't know what to say.

Neither did I.
I never know what to say.

As the elevator door opens,
I avoid the stretcher and tell myself:

this dead body used to be someone's mother,
grandmother, father, grandfather,

this dead body is just another day, another dollar
in a place full of people waiting to die.

My mother's wife pulls out hand sanitizer and
I reach for some but there isn't enough sanitizer in
the world to erase the realization of mortality.

As everyone shuffles inside the elevator,
we are unsure of the etiquette:

do we hold the door for the stretcher?
is there room for all of us in here,
including death?

Awkward, panicked eye contact ensues
in this small box of strangers.

Nobody reaches for the button to stop
the door from closing.

My mother's wife lets out a sigh of relief
as The Deacon waves his hand at us through
the closing doors.

"Go on ahead, we'll take the next one."

The Body of Christ

The Catholic Church says they are unable to make
the Body of Christ gluten-free

but my father never took the Eucharist because he
was divorced and my mother never took the
Eucharist because she was gay.

(As a child, the nuns hit her while she kneeled on
uncooked rice. "That's when I first learned
never to trust adults," she said.)

I never took the Eucharist because nobody, God or
otherwise, was really looking out for me

and I never dipped my fingers in holy water because,
oh my god, a congregation of germs was inside that
copper bowl

and I never understood why they tried to raise me to
believe in a God that didn't accept any of us.

The closest thing I have to religion is the Virgin Mary
Prayer card from my grandmother's funeral

tucked in a small jewelry case
with four tiny worry dolls
and a Klonopin

(in case of an emergency).

(RIP) WeHo Jesus

We were on the corner when she asked a man
dressed as Jesus if she could take his picture.

She was always asking everyone
if she could take their picture.

He had a latte in his hand and asked me
to hold it as he pulled a comb out of his robe
to run through his long hair & beard.

I knew him from a distance:
everyone called him West Hollywood Jesus.

He owned the building across the street and
waved like a Kennedy at us neighbors when
he drove by in his Mercedes.

Once a week, his holy robes would
hang to dry at the entrance of his building.

His tenants had to duck through them as if
it were perfectly natural to have the
Son of God as your landlord.

"Okay, I'm ready," Jesus said,
and she snapped his picture
while I held his latte,

thinking to myself:
Jesus looks good as a blonde.

Former Vet

I watched a man my age with a cardboard
sign that read: former vet.

I felt his sadness.

I watched a nurse in pink scrubs light
a cigarette and exhale.

I felt her anxiety.

I watched a teenage couple hold hands
and kiss as if they were alone.

I felt their simplicity.

I watched an old man with a cap
clutching a small bag of groceries.

I felt his solitude.

And when the bus arrived
and swept them away,

I saw nothing and felt
sadness replaced by relief.

Akashic Records

I wanted to name this book:

"Some days I feel the sanctity of my own breath
and some days I feel like a cliché paralyzed by my
own loneliness"

but my Akashic Records reader said I need to learn
to love myself, intensely and unconditionally,

to love myself the way
a mother loves her child.

"But not like your mother," she said,
"like other people's mothers."

I recalled my grandmother stirring soup on
the stove and shouting accusingly at her daughter:

"How could you leave your children?
All five of them! She was just a baby."

The *she* in that sentence is me
and it was a small kitchen, overcrowded

with my mother's guilt, my grandmother's anger,
and my urgency to become invisible.

We were grown up by then, my brothers and sisters,
we understood why our mother made her choice

(to leave and get clean or die)

but my grandmother had already
started losing her mind.

When you lose your mind
boundaries suddenly disappear,

other people's feelings become irrelevant,
time is non-linear.

You haven't left the house in five years
but yesterday was your honeymoon.

Earlier this morning, your dead sister
called on the telephone.

Tonight, you're going dancing at the old VFW hall.

Last night, your husband wasn't your
husband of fifty-two years, he was an intruder
you tried to give a black eye

but still, he stays up all night to watch you sleep.

My point is:
everyone tells you to love yourself
but they never tell you *how*

and what the fuck
are the Akashic Records anyway?

Tarot

She pulled a card from
the top of the deck and said,

"Someone from your past is going to return."

"But I don't want someone from my past
to return. I *never* want someone from my
past to return," I complained.

"Too bad," she said
and pulled another.

Author Bio:

I'm the kind of girl
you pretend to
never have kissed.

Author Bio:

Only prays
when she's
desperate.

Author Bio:

I'm an optimist
disguised as a pessimist

waiting for you
to think I'm more

than just okay,

...okay?

Author bio:

I want you to worship me
like an ancient deity

entire civilizations once
prayed to

or like an Instagram model
with at least

one million followers.

Author Bio:

I liked you so much
I had to go home

with another guy
that night at the party.

Author Bio:

I like watching you
watch me undress.

Author Bio:

I want to over romanticize
you into a different person

and then complain
to my friends about

how disappointed
I am.

Author Bio:

I spend too much time
in the company
of men

thinking
of other women.

Author bio:

I miss you a lot
but not enough to
ever speak to you again.

Author Bio:

I always have
strong sexual
chemistry with
men I can't stand.

Author Bio:

I'm standing
at your doorstep

holding a bouquet
of your past lovers.

Don't
make me
text you first.

Author Bio:

Desperate for romance.
Desperate for space.

Author Bio:

Hasn't fallen asleep
next to a member

of the opposite sex
in at least two years.

Author Bio:

will learn another language
and travel across the world
just to kiss you.

Piano Story #1

I was barely nineteen when I arrived alone
in San Francisco. The first thing I did was
get a free piano off an old woman who
didn't want to move it herself.

I didn't have a mattress,
pillows, blankets, a dresser,
a desk, or even a lamp
but I *needed* this piano.

The old woman said:
you pay me for the movers
and it's yours.

So I wrote her a check
and even though it bounced,
the piano arrived:

dusty and glorious
and out of tune.

I had no idea how to play (still don't)
but I lined the top with candles
from the dollar store, painted flowers
across the old wooden bench,

and impatiently waited for someone
to come along and make it sing.

Piano Story #2

I told you I fell in love with you that day you opened the door and Beethoven drifted from the record player behind you. We locked eyes and my heart raced as you invited me inside.

I said I loved the piano but never could play it. Well, that's not totally true...it took me a week but I once learned the opening lines of *Moonlight Sonata*.

Would you like me to play for you the opening lines of *Moonlight Sonata?*

(There's a piano maker in Massachusetts who once argued that nobody has heard the famous piece the way Beethoven meant for it to be heard. It's as if the sonata is a poem that we collectively have read and loved for centuries but the actual meaning has been completely misunderstood.

What the piano maker means is actually quite technical.

A modern piano isn't elegant enough for Beethoven's translation of *Moonlight Sonata*. The melancholic first movement is meant to be played with the sustain pedal pressed down lightly to allow the melodies to melt into each other like two lovers drifting to sleep.

The piano maker argues that the pedal on a modern piano could never initiate such delicacy, such intimacy. When the pianist presses upon it, the sound is too heavy and the notes last too long, like a guest overstaying his welcome. The piano maker argues that though the notes are the same, the meaning, the emotion, the soul of it is different.

What if one were to pause and live a lifetime in the first measures of *Moonlight Sonata* and hear it as it was meant to be heard, feel it as Beethoven and that piano maker in Massachusetts wished?

Isn't that what I want of you?
Isn't that what you want of me?

To be heard the way we feel
we were meant to be heard?)

When I told you I fell in love with you that day the record player quietly hummed *Moonlight Sonata*, you let me down gently, like the keys of a 17th century Viennese piano. Or like a man whose mother taught him how to properly treat a woman (even an undesired one).

So I move on from you and that day at your doorstep but my love affair with the piano continues.

Strongly

He once said sometimes he loves
so strongly the love feels like sadness

and he's been managing loneliness
with made-up superstitions:

like tying a string around his wrist,
thinking it might hold him together.

(*I wanted to hold him together.*)

He said give Steinbeck a chance,
all good things start out slow.

He said, look at you, you're so beautiful,
so elegant, even when you cry.

He said this as he was hurting me
but he couldn't stop hurting me.

He had traveled hundreds of miles for me
and then I watched him fall in love with
my friend instead.

He had stopped saying things to me
because he was saying them to someone else.

Heartbroken: I tied a string around my wrist
and came to know intimately of a love
so strong it could be mistaken as sadness.

Everyone's Favorite Love Poem

Way before we knew
what this was about

I chose you and you chose me:

yes, we had our other lives
and we chose those, too

every person,
every struggle
every heartache mistake
was meant to happen

so it could lead me to you
and you to me

(each other's favorite person).

Wild Hair

It was my first week in Chicago
and you asked me in front of all
my new coworkers if I was bisexual.

I gave a blurry answer
and for some reason told the story of my date
coming out of the closet on prom night.

A few days later, we stood side by side,
counting loose change in our cash registers
and you said (with your wild hair & ripped tights)

that you fingerfucked a girl the night before
and there's nothing hotter than making a girl cum.

I was unsure of your intentions
but responded quietly

that
I couldn't
agree more.

The Kind of Famous Poet

He messaged me and said, "Excuse me but do you know me? I'm kind of a famous Poet."

I didn't know him. "I thought all the famous poets were dead," I told him.

"I saw you across the room at a reading in Chicago," He continued. "You were very beautiful in an esoteric kind of way."

He told me to google him and I told him I was a writer too but he didn't seem to care much.

A few months later, the kind of famous Poet reached out again. We were both in New York and he invited me to a hip literary event in Williamsburg. This was right before Brooklyn became what people think of Brooklyn now.

I showed up at the reading wearing a low cut, backless bodysuit and a long, floral red skirt I had borrowed from my best friend. If you saw this outfit, you would understand how amazing it was.

I also was at the tail end of a nervous breakdown and was nervous breakdown skinny that year.

What I mean is: I looked good that night.
Stunning almost.

(I was always most desired when my body
was just bones and my brain too nervous for food.)

Feeling confident and stunning almost, I walked into
the event, tapped the kind of famous Poet on the
shoulder and introduced myself. He looked nervous
breakdown skinny, too.

He shook my hand, said very little and promptly ig-
nored me. He sat in front of me and next to him was
his actually famous movie star friend. She had just
written a self-help book. Why are movie stars always
writing books?

As the other writers stood up to read, I watched the
Poet sanitize his hands nine times. I memorized the
back of his greying, kind of famous head.

When it was his turn (he was the "main attraction")
the bearded host introduced him. The Poet pulled
out his book with its favorable *New York Times* review
and began to read.

To be honest, I didn't understand or care for his
work. I had bought the book after he first messaged
me and it hadn't moved me.

It's pretty easy to move me. I'm like thin glass with a
crack already making its way through. I like to cry
reading of other's misfortunes and compare and con-
trast them to my own.

During the Poet's reading the audience was silent but the bartender began collecting empty bottles, clinking them and throwing them into the trash. It was quite loud.

The bearded host got red in the face and said through gritted teeth, "Hey, can you please stop doing that? We are in the middle of a poetry reading."

The bartender must've been having a bad day because he shouted, "You're all a bunch of pretentious literary assholes!"

He wasn't wrong, though. It had been two hours and not one New York "elite" writer had acknowledged my presence.

The Poet paused and then continued to read from his book over the clinking of empty beer bottles but his confidence had faltered. His voice was less steady. He'd lost our attention.

A minute later there was shouting: a scuffle and a bang and a breaking of glass behind us.

Every pretentious literary asshole's head turned around. The bearded host of the evening had punched the bartender or maybe the bartender punched the bearded host. Somebody now had broken eyeglasses.

The Poet closed his book and sanitized his hands. That was that. We all emptied the bar and stood outside, unsure of what to do. I didn't recognize the the famous Actress but gave her a copy of my not famous book anyway. She probably threw it in the trash.

Despite my low cut, backless leotard, my borrowed long red skirt and nervous breakdown skinny physique, the Poet continued to pretend I didn't exist.

Maybe he thought I was ugly now.

Maybe I look better in a dark bar from across the room.

Maybe he has no idea how to talk to women.

Maybe something unspeakable had happened only moments before I walked through the door.

(*It's not always about you, now, is it?*)

Finally, he asked if I wanted to go to a bar with him and the Actress while admitting he didn't drink. I didn't drink either but I used to pretend to sip on a beer to make men feel more comfortable in my company.

I'm 30 now. I've stopped pretending to be whoever people think I should be.

I wandered behind the Poet and the Actress on that hot summer night, thinking how only in New York would a poetry reading end in a fist fight and only a kind of famous Poet would invite a girl he thought was esoterically beautiful somewhere and then ignore her.

None of that mattered though. The day before, I had said *I love you* for the first time over the phone to my new boyfriend, an artist an embarrassing number of years younger than me.

We had known each other only three weeks and I was about to move to Los Angeles so he could ruin my life.

Platonic Sleepover

It was a platonic sleepover. I declared it while sitting in the dark on his piano bench, eating cold Thanksgiving mashed potatoes.

"We can't kiss. I'm not kissing boys right now."

He said, "Of course not. No way, Franki. You're so ridiculous. Why would I want to kiss you?"

It was nearly 5AM. He threw his coat on the ground by his bedroom door and there was an unmistakable smell of cigarettes and sweat. He lit some incense and put on a Karen Dalton record without even turning on a light.

He asked me if I had heard of her before, she was Dylan's favorite (I hadn't) and if I wanted pajamas (I didn't).

And we tucked ourselves in. Two blankets on top, too many pillows, the fan turned on high for the sake of white noise despite it being the dead of winter.

"It's hard to keep your distance when you're stuck in a twin size bed," I mumbled while he curled an arm around me, his breath on my neck.

He was always doing this sort of thing, making me feel like I might actually matter. He'd even written a couple of songs about me and sang them off key at open mics around the city.

There was some silence as we shuffled around uncomfortably, our bodies touching but not quite sexually.

After we had settled, he whispered, "You know, you're so fucked up. You may be the most fucked up girl I know."

I tried to pull away but the bed was *so* small.

"What do you mean? How am I fucked up?" He was the one with a heart condition and still drinking, still smoking.

"I mean it as a compliment. As the best compliment you will ever receive. It's just...I know the way you see people and the way you write about them. It's too honest." He paused for a minute and then repeated himself. "It's just fucked up. What are you going to say about me? How do you see me?"

People are as turned on as they are terrified at the idea of existing in someone else's art, of being written about. I supposed they should be. We can't help ourselves.

A moment is more than just a moment, we don't let them easily pass.

(I think of that Parisian secretary I read about in *The New Yorker* who spent two decades politely writing letters to photographers, asking them to take her photo.

Her letters simply said: *"J'aimerais m'apercevoir à travers votre regard,"* or, "I would like to see myself from your point of view.")

I told him it didn't matter what I thought, who cares? We argued about it for a few minutes before he pressed himself closer to me. Kissed my shoulder. There was his breath on my neck again.

No, not going to do it. I'm not kissing boys right now.

And we fell asleep that way. Him telling me I was fucked up and me being annoyed but still less than inches apart from him on that childish bed.

All I could think was, what am I doing here? Why was I in Lincoln Park? Why was I here, in his bed, when he was always choosing other girls over me? Can anyone tell me what was so great about those other girls?

But I was 25 and I didn't know any better. It hadn't occurred to me yet to let go of people who weren't worth my attention. Like the Parisian secretary, I just wanted someone to see me, if only for the night.

He had just started to snore when he pulled me against his chest and said, "I love you."

"What did you say?"

I thought maybe it was a dream.

"I love you."

"Are you awake?" I elbowed him and he smiled softly.

"Yes. I'm awake."

Then he rolled away and began breathing deeply. I knew he wouldn't remember this in the morning. I knew this felt just like a moment in a movie, the kind you wished would happen to you.

I also knew that if I actually thought hard about it, I didn't want him or his love, real or not. I wanted a love that made it impossible for me to breathe.

Barely two hours had passed and I couldn't sleep with all the snoring and body heat and misplaced emotions.

I pushed the covers aside, quietly pulled on my boots and coat, and slipped out the door for the train station.

The Inner Monologue of a One Night Stand

The guy you think you are in love with, the one you think you've been in love with for eight years, has been on tour all summer with a massive pop star, and he's just told you he's fucked more women in the past few months than he can remember.

Three years ago you kissed (once). He was so nervous and hurt from his ex that he stopped you when you tried to reach your hand inside his jeans. You really wanted to reach your hand inside his jeans.

Two years ago, he told you he was probably in love with you but you had a boyfriend and he's politely never mentioned it again.

You had been thinking about him all summer, thinking he was the only good guy out there and how finally you were both single but now you feel a bit deceived after receiving his news. He is coming home soon and now you are less excited, less charmed, less interested. Suddenly, he feels like everyone else.

On a whim, you decide to text the person you've been sporadically sleeping with. He replies surprisingly fast and invites you over to his place.

You've never been there before so you ask for an address, leave the party you're at and head home to shave your legs in the sink. (note: are you even living if you haven't had to speed shave your legs in the sink before seeing someone who desires you?)

This person you've been sporadically sleeping with is someone who isn't really in your life but also isn't totally out of your life. He's a parenthesis, actually.

Your friends don't know anything about him, though they allude to the nameless, faceless men you have casually mentioned with raised brows while complaining about their boring boyfriends.

The guy you are about to see was very intentionally chosen for a quick hook up three months ago because you had completely cut off contact with your serious boyfriend. When the whole ordeal was finally over, you had dramatically convinced yourself nobody would ever sleep with (or love) you again. So you made a goal for yourself: to sleep with at least one or three people, you know, to move on.

"Time to move on," like the song says.

The problem is you don't know of anyone to sleep with. Since you've had a boyfriend you had stopped paying attention to any men around you and you aren't as confident as you used to be. So you find this guy through a popular hook up app that most single people have downloaded and deleted and downloaded again on their phones, an app that you declare has destroyed romance.

The guy you choose on there is tall and cute. He likes sports (you think). He wears flip-flops. No, he doesn't like to read and he can't remember the last time he had been to a concert but that's perfect. You want someone like this, someone who isn't a musician or a writer. Someone who isn't your type. You want someone different than you.

Turns out he wants someone different than him, too. To him, you are a hipster, an artsy girl, a weirdo, and that turns him on a little bit.

When he asks you what you are looking for, you simply reply: transient validation through sex and he laughs at your honesty.

So after a string of flirty texts, you decide to meet at that lame bar on Hollywood. You find him attractive but conversation is whatever and after less than an hour, you leave. To your surprise, he texts you afterward saying he wished he had kissed you.

What the hell, you think, this is why you met him in the first place, right? You daringly invite him straight to your little apartment, saying:

the door is open, come in, take a right at the end of the hall and don't speak, just start fucking me.

Thinking back, you're lucky you didn't get killed.

But this is something you have wanted to do all your life and you've always been a fan of fulfilling fantasies. Turns out he is a good listener. He arrives quietly, enters your room, immediately kicks off his shoes and pulls off his shirt as you watch from your bed. Pretty soon his lips, his body are on you.

He doesn't even fumble when he puts on the condom, he's that smooth.

And so you two fuck.

It all happens in less than twenty minutes.

He didn't even say hello.

He doesn't say goodbye either because that wasn't part of the plan (no talking) but as he leaves, he places another condom on your desk and says, "That's for next time."

To this day, that is still one of the hottest things a guy has said to you. You didn't expect to actually talk again, his purpose now served, but you are both so blown away by how hot it was that you stay in touch.

You are both out of town a lot and have opposite schedules, but you manage to meet again.

That night, the sex is just as good and you realize he is actually fun to talk to. He is surprised by how cool he finds you. This happens a few more times with months in between. Since you don't like him and have nothing in common, you can go weeks without texting and not give a shit at all. Tonight at the party is one of those nights you decide to talk again.

You text him and he says right away:
come over.

You haven't seen him in awhile but you've been so busy with work and horny that this feels like a good idea. Because it's LA, the electricity is randomly out on your entire block. So here you are, shaving your legs in the sink by candlelight and putting on lacy black underwear. You decide not to wear a bra. You drive to his apartment and are surprised to find that he lives in a modern condo surrounded by palm trees, bougainvilleas and other equally fancy condos.

The air on this side of town is distinctly warmer than in your neighborhood. When he lets you in, you enter what can only be described as a bachelor pad. There is nothing in the living room except for a grey leather couch and a massive TV.

He offers you a water and courteously pours it in a glass as you watch and make small talk. You feel like he has his shit together because he uses a Brita filter. He looks cute and although he is going a little bit bald, you don't mind. He is wearing flip-flops, something you made fun of him for before, basketball shorts and a tee shirt with the Nike logo.

He looks like the guy next door. He's all-American, the kind of guy who would've never acknowledged you in high school.

You notice how sterile the place is, not a single piece of clutter, not even a piece of mail or a misplaced shoe. Nothing on the walls. You search for signs of what kind of person he might actually be.

This is something you notice every time you talk. He is impossible to get to know and also doesn't want to get to know you. Maybe this is on purpose. There's a wall and you accept that because you are/he is just a fling.

The only book he owns is yours, which he secretly bought online after the first time he met you.

He never told you if he liked it so you assume he didn't read it, didn't understand it or didn't care for it. You always wanted someone to fall in love with you solely from reading one of your stories but it hasn't happened. There's certain people you truly believe should be in love with you but they aren't.

It's eerily quiet as you sit down in his apartment, so quiet that you can hear that constant white noise that is stuck in your ears from all the loud concerts you've attended over the years.

Somehow, you begin talking about his "career." Which is second photography assistant for reality TV shows and commercials. You ask him what the end game is, what he wants to do, because everyone in LA wants to do something big.

He isn't sure. Says maybe he will be a producer and when you ask him what that means, he gives an evasive answer. You don't like guys who don't have impossibly large goals but this doesn't matter:

you are/he is just a fling.

You tell him maybe one day you will work in television too and with great delusion of grandeur you talk about all the TV shows you would like to be writing for. It seems, you think, that the universe owes you this. A paycheck for being a writer. Because why not?

Then you admit, as you sip on the filtered water, that the problem is you don't have any fucking ideas. *What good is a writer without any ideas?* You ask. He laughs for the first time and you start to feel comfortable.

You cross your legs on his couch and then realize the leather is too nice for that and put them back down. You touch his arm and tell him he's so normal; he doesn't even have any tattoos. You mention you want to get another and he doesn't ask you of what, just where.

You get up to use the bathroom and while washing your hands, you think to yourself how wonderful it is to be young and in Los Angeles and in this apartment with such an all-American dude, about to have hot sex. We're all adults here now. You feel like you are watching this scene unfold from afar instead of being the main character.

You return and ask him to put some music on and after laughing at the few playlists he has made on his phone, you quickly pull together a couple of sexy albums, and finally the mood is set.

You ask him to kiss you.

He jokes and says, "I thought you just came here to hang out."

And then he kisses you.

You can tell he is already hard through his flimsy basketball shorts (you have never been friends with the kind of guy who wears basketball shorts) and he leads you into his bedroom. There, he lights a candle and you have to reset the mood by playing music on your phone.

His bedroom is just as empty as the rest of his apartment and you glance around trying to find some sign of his personality. You feel as if you are in a catalogue for a furniture company. He asks you if you think his pillowcases should be grey instead of white. The whole room, his carpet, his bedspread, his walls are grey and you call him a bachelor.

He stretches out, all masculine and confident, already naked on top of his sheets. He watches you undress and calls you a hipster, with your skinny jeans, as you struggle to slide them off.

There's nothing more to talk about so you walk over to the bed, let your lips hesitate for a moment in front of his, and then kiss. He's admitted to you before he's "not really a fan of foreplay" but you try to tease him anyway.

You climb on top of him, your knee between his thighs, pushing rhythmically as you kiss his neck.

You make sure not to be sloppy with your mouth. You bite his bottom lip, you bite his nipples maybe a little too hard and work your way down. You kiss his torso in a way that makes his whole body arch toward you. He is quiet so it's difficult to tell if he likes any of this.

You listen to his body instead.

When you finally go down on him, you make note that he has shaved down there and his hand is on your head trying to push himself deeper, faster. You slap him away and your slap says, "I'm in control."

He has barely touched you but by the time you're done, you're so wet it doesn't matter. He slips a condom on, again, smooth as fuck.

You start having sex.

He's on top of you and really, it all feels very passionate. The kind of sex that could trick you into thinking it means something if you aren't careful.

He goes really slow this time and he doesn't feel as hard as before and you think to yourself that probably means 1) he thinks you are gross and ugly or 2) he's trying not to cum too soon. This works in your favor because the pace is achingly slow, which is how you like to have sex, and after a few minutes you reach your hand between your thighs and tell him to go faster.

It isn't long before you cum, hard.

In the back of your head, you think of your girl friends that say they can't orgasm without an emotional connection and you think of that article on the *Huffington Post* that says there is no actual proof there is a g-spot and most women can't have an orgasm during sex. You are grateful that none of these things pertain to you.

In fact, the opposite is happening.

Every person you have slept with in the past year has been able to make you cum on the first or second try and quite easily.

You attest this not to your sexual prowess or their skills but mostly due to the fact that:

1) you know how to use your hand
2) you're a good teacher and
3) you had thrown away your last bottle of Lexapro.

This, you think, is your reward for spending weeks in withdrawal, dizzy and nauseous as you weaned yourself off the drug. The drug that made you tired and asexual. The drug that turned your rail thin body into curves that you disdain. But it's also the drug that saved your life when three years ago going to places like the convenient store or riding the train seemed like impossible feats, and you could only eat a tiny list of "safe" foods.

You want to bask in these small orgasmic victories now in case the panic attacks return, in case the depression returns, in case your shitty life returns, and you hope that they won't because you've (*mostly*) gotten over your past and your fears and you worked really hard to do that.

After you orgasm, he asks you if you came, which annoys you because it's quite obvious and then he is suddenly super hard, poking at your g-spot that the *Huffington Post* claims doesn't exist, and you moan encouragingly while he asks you where he should cum.

"On my tits," you say like a good girl playing bad. He pulls off the condom and once again, is a great listener.

When he stands up and leaves the room to get you a towel, you turn to your left, where you realize the closet is actually a massive mirrored door.

You look at your face and then your breasts and your stomach and your thighs as you cringe. You adjust your legs and arms in a way that might make you look skinnier, sexier but it's hard to look cute with a puddle of cum all over you.

You give up. This is your body. This is how you look.

You remember he once told you being insecure was a major turn off yet he's never called you hot, he's never called you funny or smart, he's never called you anything that might provide the fleeting validation one seeks from a meaningless lover.

Finally, he hands you a towel and then goes back into the bathroom for what seems like an hour, washing off his dick. Then you go in there and wash yourself too and pray that you don't get a UTI because that's how your body punishes you when you have sex with someone you probably aren't supposed to.

You return to the bedroom and minor cuddling ensues where you scratch his back and he wraps his arms around you.

This is your favorite part, you think. Not cuddling but the conversation that follows an orgasm. This is when the wall goes down.

But the mood shifts.

Of course, it does.

He mentions that he would never date a girl who he slept with the first night he met her and that most guys wouldn't. He says it makes her less desirable and makes guys want to put less effort in. He only likes girls who make him wait. All guys, he says, think like this.

Obviously, he has slept with you the first night so this feels a little awkward. You roll through the list of men you have dated and whether or not you slept with them the first night.

You ask him if he's ever been in love and when was the last time he had a serious girlfriend and the answer is yes, in high school he was in love (you say that doesn't count) and his last girlfriend was 6 years ago, when he was 22 (also doesn't count).

You say it's obvious he has never been in love solely because he doesn't understand foreplay and you are feeling a little offended that he has lumped you into a category of women he wouldn't date (even though you don't want to date him either) and wonder what other guys have lumped you into this category (probably everyone).

You remember last month how he wouldn't fuck you because you were on your period and vaguely wonder: is he a misogynist?

He talks about how he once met a girl who he thought could be THE ONE; she had all these perfect qualities.

She was a teacher and liked to run and do yoga and cook and paint her nails to match his favorite sports teams and you wonder if his dick had really just been inside of you.

You don't know how to steer the conversation away from this and start to feel beside the point.

Then he asks you about the new guy you like, an Australian composer, and you try not to give many details. You stupidly had mentioned him at some point in the past few weeks. He is fishing to see if you have slept with him and you don't want to answer. This suddenly isn't feeling fun at all. The vibe is off. You feel inelegant and like an idiot. You feel like, let's just go ahead and say it, a slut.

Your immediate reaction is to flee.

Fight or flight.

Somehow, the conversation takes an even worse turn and he starts talking about his penis and how girls love his size. You instantly think to yourself *how many girls?* and you find yourself assessing out loud your own stupid fucking opinions on penis size and he is probably thinking to himself *how many guys?* if he's thinking anything at all.

(emphasis on:
if he's thinking anything at all).

It is the least intimate conversation you can have with someone you have just been intimate with: lying there talking about other people you've slept with and other people you like more than the person you are with.

Suddenly, you feel very alone. You are the most alone person in the entire world.

(Earlier, you had applauded yourself for being so sexually free. Now, you scold yourself for being in this situation, for giving life to this sort of relationship and conversation.

This is a constant push and pull for you: wanting to be sexually free and not giving a fuck but also wanting to take your time, to save yourself for someone who deserves it, who has earned it, to attract something more meaningful into your life.

But the bottom line is: you're better than this.

This is worse than that empty feeling you had earlier today at the hair salon where the woman next to you gushes about how excited her husband and family and sorority sisters are that she's pregnant. That was when you realized you hate everybody, you will never be happy, you can't imagine ever wanting to be a mother, you can't even imagine that feeling of what it's like to be loved, romantically or otherwise.

In fact, you keep meeting people who hate love, who don't believe in it, who avoid it, who curse it and each one of those people has taken a piece of you.)

He is lying on his back now, with one arm resting over his forehead. The candle is leaving a sinister glow on his face. By now, your vagina has dried up like the Sahara desert as your thoughts snowball.

You say you are going to leave and he doesn't even pretend to want you to stay a little longer.

You grope around the floor for your clothes, your once sexy underwear feels slimy and cold and when you find your jeans, you move to the corner by the door to put them on.

"I hate that mirror," you say to him, pointing at the closet door you are avoiding while pulling up your too tight jeans, and he says he loves it. Insecurity, it really is such a turn off.

He asks you if you are leaving and you say yes (isn't that what you just said?). Only slightly confused, he gets up and starts to dress and asks if you are parked far. He says he will walk you to your car. What a fucking gentleman.

You find your bag in his living room and head for the door while he is still pulling up those stupid basketball shorts. You're embarrassed for having emotions.

Don't be embarrassed for having emotions.

You say in a not so great tone that you don't need him to walk you out but thanks. Finally, he catches that something weird is going on and asks from across the room if everything is okay.

You have already opened the door, one foot out, but you don't want your voice to echo down the hallway so you close it for a second and pause. You can't put your finger on this feeling.

"That just wasn't very good post sex conversation," you say and shrug. You realize he has now lumped you into another category: crazy girl...(and you really could care less).

His eyes widen and he says, "Oh shit, I didn't mean to bum you out." And you leave.

You are, needless to say, bummed out. Not about him but more about yourself and your suddenly bleak future of dating, of love, of connection, of adulthood, of your lack of feminism when it comes to your dead-end relationships.

You walk to your car trying to figure out what the hell just happened. You sit behind the steering wheel trying to shake the feeling of the evening and he has already texted you. He doesn't ask why you left, just wishes you a good night in what feels like a weak attempt to salvage the past 15-20 minutes.

You start your car, put on Bob Dylan, and decide to take the long way home.

Date #1 (or never finding love)

Maybe my dress was too short
or I used the word cum too many
times in my stories

but at the end of the night
he said: "I can't kiss you because
then I will never talk to you again."

He looked wild and unsure.
I could trace his spine with my eyes
while he bent down to tie his shoes.

I could sense from his panic
that he was preparing to sprint
out of my life as quickly as he sprinted in.

After he left, I leaned against the door in
the dark thinking how there's two kinds
of girls:

there are the ones who come before you
(god, you have to be careful about what
they've done)

and the ones who come after
(they're the marrying kind)

and I'm always in between the two,
taking notes, holding my breath,
trying not to make any sudden movements.

Date #2

You were exactly my type:
thick glasses, beard,
strong vocabulary,
a little bit gay…
okay, a lot gay.

You wore a nice gold watch
and mala beads on your wrist,
a combination you never wore again.

I wore a white shirt that fell off my shoulder
and red lipstick because red lips sink ships.

We started talking about reincarnation and
you guessed my past life on the very first try.

(A reader once told me I was a woman
 who dressed as a man to be a sailor.

How the hell did you guess that?)

Then you said you didn't believe in past lives or soul
mates and that nothing really happens when we die.

This worried me only slightly, the not believing.

When you accidentally touched my arm,
we both jumped, the feeling unprecedented.

I went to the bathroom to reapply my lipstick
and text a friend about how intellectual and
sexy you were.

At the end of the night you walked me
to my car and kissed me on the sidewalk.

It was almost too perfect, this kiss:
gentle, patient, thoughtful.

When you walked away,
 my head was spinning.

I climbed into my car,
rested my head on the
steering wheel and said,

"fuck. fuck. fuck."
like a heart murmur.

I was already
falling in love with you,

why weren't you
falling in love with me?

Date #3

I blankly stare at the tattoos on his arm
while he nonchalantly mentions his great,
great grandmother was F. Scott Fitzgerald's muse.

He gives a longwinded explanation about why he
hates classical music academia and I feel as if I'm lis-
tening in on a boring lecture where the teacher could
give two shits about my opinion.

It doesn't occur to him to ask me how I've been in the
past seven years since he's seen me but he does ask
for a job (because, you know, he's a musician).

"Give me a reason to move to LA." He's the second
person to ask me to give them a reason to move to
LA but the reason isn't me.

He says after years of being "a cactus alone in a vast
desert" (*god, how original*) he finally fell in love once.

One night, he left the girl's apartment and stood out-
side her door for fifteen minutes, frozen with the un-
familiar emotion.

She didn't want him, of course, cause that's how love
works some times…most times.

I sip my water and think about how he was never
that great of a kisser and ate pussy like a surgeon
even though he could recite Dostoevsky and play
Chopin from memory.

Date #4

He tells me his whole life story and that's okay, I like to listen. He's a carpenter, a bee keeper, a painter. His mother is in a cult and his ex-girlfriend just transitioned into his ex-boyfriend. He's always at the spot on the corner cause that's where the NA meetings are. I don't flinch when he admits he's been clean of heroin for 19 months, I congratulate him.

He says with relief, "Any other girl would be judging me right now."

(What I don't say is that I grew up going to AA meetings. My father took us to them, with the instant coffee and bowls of hard candy and fluorescent lights. Why would he take his children to an AA meeting?

What I don't say is my mother has been sober over 20 years and it's not a coincidence I've never been drunk and that I worry every time I take a pill.)

At the end of the night, we hug awkwardly on the sidewalk and as I walk away he grabs my hand and pulls me back for a kiss. He says he can't believe he met me: I'm so...so everything.

Apparently, I've left him speechless. The next day, he's so enamored by the memory of our date that he makes a hand-painted card sealed with actual beeswax from his actual bees and asks for my address to mail it to me.

It's romantic, I have to admit. I'm getting caught up in all this, even though I should know better by now.

He invites me to a canyon that weekend and brings a blanket, a book of scary stories and a flashlight. We spend four hours kissing and keeping each other warm from the Santa Ana winds.

I hold his hand walking back to his vintage car because, of course, he has a vintage car, the beater type without any seat belts or a radio. I feel confident for once; I feel he really likes me to have put in such an effort for a second date.

A week goes by. No word from him. I mean, of course not.

This time, I've left him speechless in the unfavorable way. I wonder to myself, how do you kiss someone for four hours and not think of them?

During his silence, his beeswax sealed card arrives in the mail. Inside is a shitty half poem in calligraphy that says how kismet it is to have found me.

I set aside some of my dignity and send him a casual text. He writes back instantly but the tone is dismissive. "I don't want a girlfriend, it's not you! (LOL) I don't want to date ANYONE."

I look up the word kismet to make sure I've got the right definition.

Then I look up the word presumptuous.

All I had said was, "What's up?" I just wanted to get to know him, *then* decide if we liked each other.

I try to figure out what happened, concocting a narrative about myself from his point of view.

Maybe he got high off of meeting me the way he would get high off drugs. A high is never as good as the first time, is it? Maybe I talked too much about books or bands or wanting a nose job.

Or maybe I should stop thinking of all the things "wrong" with me every time a guy I'm not even that interested in swan dives from hot to cold.

Now, when I see him standing outside the NA meeting smoking a cigarette or at a concert or waiting at the crosswalk, I wave and pretend not to remember his name until I really, truly, honestly can't remember.

Date #5 (or Silver Lake Lounge)

The bar is lit with nauseating green lights and a unicorn head is mounted on the wall.

It's the kind of place where the bathroom has no mirror or toilet paper. Someone has scrawled
"too short to box with god" across the broken door.

The band on stage is taking themselves so seriously. There's a tall guy standing in front of me with his friends and he looks like you. Or he looks like a watered down version of you.

This guy in front of me is probably a little more relaxed, a little less handsome. He has the same pout as you, the same glasses, but probably plays video games instead of pondering over pages of *The Illiad*.

I kind of want to kiss him only to simulate kissing you. I used to want to kiss you, you know. At least in the beginning, don't worry, not anymore, not really.

I debate introducing myself to the simulacrum of you but I write him a note on an old receipt instead:

I hope you're not a coward like the rest of us.

As I walk out the door, I tap him on the shoulder with the receipt and say,

"I think you dropped this."

Date #6

We had been dating awhile now,
a year and a half in that grey area where
I wasn't allowed to say what I felt because
he wouldn't say what he felt.

I finally asked:
"Don't you want to care about somebody?
Don't you want somebody to care about you?"

He covered his face with his hands
and groaned: "Being cared about is
SUCH a responsibility."

He told me he could never be in
a monogamous relationship again but
I knew he just didn't want to get hurt.

(suddenly it occurred to me that I was
Basically dating a child.)

I asked: "How can you love two people
when you can't even love one?"

And what a super power he must have,
never needing another person

and what a lonely super power
that must be.

Date #7

My last night in Italy:
he's my waiter.
It's instant, our attraction.

We can't keep our eyes off
each other. After he takes
my order, he walks past me,
again and again,
flashing secret smiles.

We don't speak the same
language but we figure it out.

I point to my tattoo
and say Picasso,
he points to his
and says Hunter S. Thompson.

Art and artists are our
universal language.

I wait for him to get off work,
by then it's midnight and we walk
to the darkened sea.

I have one poem left in my pocket
and I give it to him.

It reads in Italian:

I believe in fate...on a good day.

(Lo credo nel destino
nelle giornate buone).

In broken English
he says he believes
this could be fate,

I believe this could be fate
too (at least for tonight).

There's a lightning storm
without rain
and with hashish
and warm lips

we don't need words,
just hands, to get to know
each other.

Date #8

We meet in front of the Notre Dame
during sunset, the perfect time to look into
a stranger's eyes. He's shy and dressed so formally
with his button down shirt tucked into trousers.

I had spent the day wandering the tunnels of the cat-
acombs, wondering about the 6 millions souls of the
6 million skeletons stacked beneath Paris.

He talks of history as we walk along the Seine until
we stumble into a bookstore as it's closing.

I gasp when I see a display dedicated to Richard
Brautigan because nobody knows Richard Brautigan.

I show him the book *In Watermelon Sugar* while
pointing to my *In Watermelon Sugar* tattoo. English is
his second or third language so it takes him a minute
to realize before he smiles in surprise. I tell him he
has a lovely smile.

While I'm upstairs, he buys me a book I've never
heard of and when I ask him his favorite, he blushes
hard and says grew up studying math, too busy to
read.

At the end of the night, he takes my hand and says,

"I don't understand what American boys did to
make you hate love, Franki. It's not so bad."

Date #9 (Ojos Azules / Blue Eyes)

He had a large wooden rosary
around his neck but fuck-me eyes
that wanted to follow me inside.

Earlier that night, he had driven me
to the top of Bogota and we stood on a cliff
while he spoke of his love of Colombia.

I'd only known him a few hours
but I could tell he was meant to
pass on some sort of wisdom to me.

At the end of the night, I kissed him
in his car without hesitation.

I'd never been so sure of a kiss before.

When he followed me inside, I sat on the bed
and he knelt on the ground, as if in prayer,
and said with his Colombian accent:

"I want you to understand why I'm a Christian."

His spoke of poverty, of family, of faith,
of being saved.

His sincerity made my heart ache
like a muscle seldom used.

I had never met anyone who had found a God
that had been kind to them, a God who had given

them a reason to believe instead of just
expecting it of you.

I held back tears as he said:

"Ojos Azules, if you could see yourself
through my eyes, you'd never have a
bad day again."

This near stranger saw more behind those eyes
than all the men who never deserved my body,
who never deserved my thoughts.

He saw who I was right in that moment
and he saw who I could be.

"You don't even know what the world has planned
for you," He said. "But I do. Don't worry, Blue Eyes."

For a near virgin, his touch was maniacal versus my
slow sensuality: together we were calm meets storm,
we were contained chaos.

After, as the dawn painted the window from black to
navy, I watched him dress.

He turned my way and said,
"I don't want to be forgotten by you."

It's a sentiment I had come across a lot
in this country and it was quite beautiful.

(Your wish came true, I won't ever forget)

The look in his eyes changed when I said:

"I just fell in love with you for three hours
and forty-five minutes."

I liked the idea of a love that had an easy start and
finish, a clear expiration date, a love that didn't have
to end up in flames.

When I left Colombia I carried back with me
something I'm afraid to say out loud because
I know I'm going to lose it.

I'm going to go back to Los Angeles and make the
wrong choices again because of my impatience and
because of my loneliness.

I'm going to let the wrong people in
because I don't know where to find
the right people especially when
the wrong people feel like the right
people (at first).

But what he had given me was: hope.

A very simple but strong hope:

in love, in a god, in family, in him, in myself,
in my writing, in the future, in the people
I have met and have yet to meet.

And now that he's gone,
I'm desperately trying to hold onto it.

How To Get a Guy to Cook You Dinner

Follow these steps carefully:

Meet him at the Echo Park bar that you met your ex boyfriend at three years ago on your first day in Los Angeles. Find him in the corner with a giant sleeping doberman. (You can't believe they let the dog into the bar but it's LA.)

Talk about his tattoos and find out you both have a Kurt Vonnegut tattoo. Try to feign your excitement because the last guy who asked you out two weeks ago also had a Kurt Vonnegut tattoo. (These guys are a dime a dozen. You're a dime a dozen.)

Find out he was in a band that toured with a lot of bands you worked with but then he acts weird and doesn't want to tell you the name of his band. Realize he's probably lying to you. Tell him you work in the music industry because everybody in publishing said your writing is too uncomfortable to be marketable.

Immediately get in a strange, abrasive fight by accidentally saying you are trying not to date any struggling musicians. Be accused of being both condescending and a hypocrite because you are an aspiring writer.

Reminder:

Men don't like when you are condescending toward them.

Slight subject change. He asks you your favorite bands and you hesitate and say, "probably nothing you would like." He scoffs and finally you say *"War on Drugs"* which feels like a safe choice and he says he hates them.

There's a long silence where you both look at the dog, who doesn't give a fuck.

Excuse yourself. Go to the bathroom, look in the mirror and ask yourself: should I leave? I should leave.

Go back to the corner with the tattooed boy and sleeping doberman and say: "So, we aren't really getting along. I'm gonna head out."

His face will fill with surprise. He will ask you to stay and spend the evening back pedaling into your good graces. You now have the upper hand. The mood shifts and suddenly he is funny and charming and maybe not so bad.

He likes Murakami, which is somewhat of a turn on even though you never could finish his books. He even tells you he acted so weird at first because you are too intelligent and intimidating, which you don't believe.

(You never want to believe anyone who says anything good about you

...why is that?)

He will walk you to your car. You let him kiss you because why the fuck haven't you found anyone yet? His touch makes your skin crawl and not in a good way. His kiss is nothing worth noting so you pull away, wipe your lips.

The next day, he will ask to cook you dinner.

(You should say no).

What About When a Woman Cooks You Dinner?

She cooked me dinner while I watched from a small table in her small kitchen, trying my hardest to act casual. I noted her paintings on the wall and how they were exactly like her: fiery and difficult to understand.

She was wearing a short dress, her hair reaching toward her waist, long legs, dirty bare feet.

I was wearing a short dress, my hair reaching toward my waist, long legs, dirty bare feet.

We had dressed for each other, our sole purpose seduction. I was both fascinated and afraid of her femininity. She used to be a model but doesn't want to talk about it. We all used to be a lot of things, didn't we?

After dinner, she put on a record, lit a candle and a joint, and pulled from under her bed a box of expensive perfumes. She told me she had sold fragrances to rich women in a fancy beach town for years, helping them mix and match scents, waxing and waning vanilla and bergamot, citrus and myrrh, hoping to concoct a purpose for their lives.

She said, "A woman's scent is part of her mythology."

*

Scientifically, it is said that when we first come across a new scent, the part of the brain that processes memory also processes smell. So at the very first inhalation, our brain forever links that scent to a person, a place, a moment.

I know this well. I've had past lovers appear out of the blue to recount the familiar linger of my perfume at the farmer's market, an airport, a health food store. Even though they are all settled down now, they talk about how it ignited a subtle fondness or longing or sadness or loss for me.

How it elicited *saudade*.

Mostly though, the unexpected return of my scent elicited nothing more than a hard-on and a failed rekindling.

*

"This is probably two thousand dollars worth of perfume," she said, pulling from the box a large, crystal bottle. She flashed a sideways smile. "Don't tell anyone."

We both watched as she sprayed the tattoo on my forearm and gently rubbed it in. Then she sprayed her own delicate collar bone and leaned forward so I could breathe her in.

All of it was so over the top sensual, so specifically lovely, the moment so female, so ours.

"I know you love amber scents but try this one," she said, handing me a small vial of rose oil. "You can keep it." I breathed in roses before tucking the small bottle into the pocket of my dress.

Her territory was now marked: rose oil and the memory of her interchangeable in that crevice of my brain that attaches scent to a person, a place, a moment.

*

Rose oil from now on sends the reminder of what it was like a few moments later to first kiss a woman, how soft and secretive it felt.

Rose oil is watching her removing her dress and kneeling before me wearing only a black choker and perfume.

Rose oil is my hands shakily discovering her perfect, small breasts, unsure of what to do even though her body is my body.

Rose oil is my first touch between her legs, her pushing my hand deeper inside of her. Rose oil is making her cum and later, myself being too nervous to.

Rose oil is her breathless smile afterward, my disbelief of having someone so exotic at my fingertips.

Rose oil is role reversal: her turning to me, saying she wants a meaningful relationship while I avoid her eyes and slip from her bed as many men have done to me before, as many men will do in the future.

Rose oil is when the first kiss is also the last.

Today is the Day

We knew each other for a couple of years before we actually spoke. I thought she was too pretty, too hip, and looked like a bitch. She didn't think much of me either. She was a musician and I was a writer and we competed for many of the same useless boys in Chicago.

At some point, we finally talked and realized we were both Capricorns, grew up in towns right next to each other in boring Indiana and wouldn't mind kissing each other. When it comes to the same sex, you sometimes tightrope walk between jealousy and desire.

We figured most of this out, I think, while sitting in the back of an empty bus on the 4th of July, heading from Pilsen to Wicker Park. Neither of us could afford a cab. We had never hung out officially before but I invited her to a party full of agonizing hipsters that didn't care to bathe or talk to us.

I remember we were both wearing short skirts, tank tops and had long hair and bangs. (I'm starting to worry that my type is just a rearrangement of myself.)

Our sweaty knees and thighs were pressing against each other in the back of that bus when she told me she sometimes kissed girls and I said I sometimes kissed girls too. I think I was fishing for it though, her gender blindness. I was probably fishing for it.

We didn't really look at each other after that but the energy changed immediately.

It was the sudden possibility of *what if?*

When we got off the bus and ended up in her loft on the 6th floor, nothing happened, though. It was over 100 degrees, probably 150 degrees inside. We sat on a couch and she rolled cigarettes as I looked outside her window at the elevated subway rattling by. The train was so close, it felt like you could reach inside and pluck the sadness right off the nameless passengers.

Maybe we wanted to kiss each other but she suddenly had a toothache that would land her in the emergency room later that night and me in my bed, alone.

We didn't see each other again until six months later on a freezing Sunday afternoon. She showed up at my door and looked beautiful in a melancholic way with her heavy bangs and blurred cat eyeliner. It was her birthday the night before and she also looked tired, hung over, maybe.

I thought back to our conversation on the bus in the summer and wondered why she was here. She took off her heavy coat and shook the snow off her boots and followed me into my bedroom. It took us a moment to get comfortable but soon we were on my bed laughing and complaining about men and getting fired and getting the hell out of Chicago.

I began to relax and have fun when suddenly, she wrapped her body in my entire bed comforter and dragged herself into the living room. Then she curled up on the couch and said, "I don't feel well."

I tried to express concern but every nerve in my body lit with small panic. I should probably mention now that there is nothing I hate more than germs. Well, germs and throwing up. In fact, I am so preoccupied with not getting sick myself that I lack the ability to take care of people.

Nurturing is the last word to describe me, I suppose.

I asked a litany of questions disguised as concern to try and diagnose her. (Did she have a sore throat, a fever or stomach pain? Was she hung over? Did you recently eat street meat or McDonald's? Do you feel sick SICK, like STOMACH FLU SICK? God, I hope not.)

She shrugged at my questions, cocooned in the blanket and said almost in a baby voice, "I don't know, I just feel really sick. Nauseous."

I measured the distance between her and I, analyzing the safety of the air between us. I began to bite my nails then stopped just as quickly, realizing I must have her germs all over my hands. As she clutched her stomach, I thought about how nobody had ever thrown up in my toilet since I moved into that apartment on Chicago Avenue and how I'd like it to stay that way.

I began to offer her any remedy I could think of for a stomachache. I had them all. Peppermint tea. Tums. Pepto Bismol. Ginger candy. Apple Cider Vinegar.
There was a period of my life where I couldn't leave the house without carrying around a bottle of Emetrol for nausea and a packet of peppermint tea in case I felt like I might throw up.

She declined my suggestions and grabbed a pillow from the corner of the couch. She tucked it under her chin and said without looking at me:

"Today is the day the man who murdered my mom gets out of jail."

She said it very nonchalantly but the words alone turned the room to ice. Of course, we weren't close enough for me to know about her mother. I had assumed that like most mothers, she was alive.

Shame washed over me. Here, I had been worrying about the flu when she had a much bigger burden on her shoulders.

Today is the day the man who murdered my mom gets out of jail.

Jesus, the weight of that sentence. What business did it have in here? Who was this devastating girl on my couch? Who was this horrible man?

What had happened?

Was I allowed to ask?

She admitted the details of it all were still patchy and unclear to her. Her family seemed to keep most of it a secret. I tried to figure out how to console her. The problem was, she seemed like she didn't need consoling.

She didn't say much but from what I could gather her mother may have been a sex worker and she may have been stabbed. She was young when she died, too young. I mean...fuck. Her sadness suddenly was my sadness.

It seemed as if she had successfully distanced herself from the mysterious death (although she had her mother's first and last name tattooed along her two fingers, revealed only when she flashed someone the "peace sign.")

Here she was, cool as a cucumber, acting as if it were no big deal, this person getting out of jail. It's a typical coping mechanism of a Capricorn, if you ask me.

She shook her head when I suggested we go back to our hometown and unearth old newspapers and figure out the truth. Visit her mother's grave. Should we hold a séance? I knew a surprising amount of legitimate psychics. I imagined her journey that was now my journey being like that movie *Now & Then*, something I could eventually turn into a best selling book and movie.

Always a writer. Never completely present.
Always a writer. Always so fucking self involved.

We were quiet as she brushed off my suggestions and to my relief, she got a phone call and soon it was time for her to catch the train. She left the blankets and pillow on my couch and tried to hug me goodbye. I held my breath in case she was actually sick and told her I hoped she felt better and that I was so sorry about her mother.

As I shut the door, I said a little prayer to whatever higher power might listen.

A few hours later, she called me to say she had gone home and thrown up several times. She couldn't stop throwing up, what should she do? I clutched the phone in sheer panic.

(I should probably mention I've been downplaying my inner monologue. The truth is, I have not thrown up since I was sixteen. That's more than a decade, knock on wood. In fact, I have only thrown up three and a half times in my entire life. I can tell you exactly what I ate and where I was. I would rather die than throw up. I can go days or weeks or months without eating much or leaving my house if I have a particularly bad spell of this anxiety.

My therapist said it all boils down to control issues from my childhood and he's right:

there is nothing scarier than losing control.)

I hung up on this poor, sick girl, took a deep breath and immediately took inventory of everything she had touched in my apartment.

The doorknob, obviously. My bed. She had been sprawled across it. She had used my computer. She had sat on the couch. The pillow and comforter. She had used the bathroom! Her teacup rested on the table with her kiss still on the edge of it. Everything was suspect of germs.

I went into the kitchen and grabbed rubber gloves and disinfecting supplies and began to clean furiously, trying to wash away both the feeling of her lost mother and the stomach flu I was no doubt bound to catch in the next 48-72 hours.

After 2 hours of cleaning, I finally felt comfortable enough to sit in my own apartment. Let's be clear: it's not a day I'm proud of. I realize now, it probably wasn't germs that made her sick, it was that evil man, the thought of him taking away her mother and then being set free. Why was he set free?

I never did catch the flu. I never did kiss her and I never found out more about her mother.

Quantum Entanglement:

When Einstein wrote of it, he was speaking of science, of physics. When the boy from London spoke of it, he was speaking of you.

To simplify: it is believed that once particles interact in such a way, they can no longer be defined as two entities. Even if these particles are separated, no matter the distance, they continue to affect each other and exist in the universe as a whole.

That is to say:
once entangled, always entangled.

The boy from London thinks this idea can be applied to love: to two souls, to two hearts. He believes this can be applied to him and to you.

No matter the distance, the mistakes, the uncertainty: your universes are still one, you continue to touch each other in the most subtle of ways.

To simplify:

He cannot and will not forget you.
Once entangled, always entangled.

Instead of almost love: always love.

How it began:

I was skinny –
nervous breakdown
skinny when we met.

I wore red lips
with a borrowed
black leather jacket.

(Two things I rarely do.)

It was 5AM at a party in LA;
I pulled you on the dance floor
and hid my own unavailability

when I said:

"You're very attractive
and it seems like you have
commitment issues."

Then I kissed the fuck out of you.

*

We fell in love
when we found out we were on
the same anti-depressants.

*

We moved in with each other
without really discussing.

First you left some clothes
and some paint brushes,

and then you put that pull-up bar
in my doorway, which I thought was
kind of hot.

It didn't matter if it was too soon,
it didn't matter what all our friends said.
We were so lucky to have found each other.

That was back when you would come home
drunk and list off all the millions of reasons why
you loved me and I listed off the millions of reasons
I loved you.

*

It felt so good to love.
This is what we are here for,
I had thought to myself,
to give and receive love.

*

We fell out of love
during that horrible heat wave
when we didn't have AC,

when you jumped out of my car
while it was still moving and
I couldn't find you,

when you got drunk
and called me a slut because of
the way I wrote,

when you tried to climb out our
two story window during a fight,

when you sat in the middle of our street
waiting but not really waiting
for a car to hit you,

when your temper started to remind me
of my father,

when you banged so hard on the bathroom
door as I thought to myself,

oh my god, I've made a horrible mistake.

How it ended:

You hated my books, you hated me.
As we drove down Sunset Blvd.,

you shouted: "And don't you DARE
write about me. I'm not just some guy in
your stories. I mean something."

I looked out the window and wondered:
how can someone save your life
and then ruin it just as easily?

my hero. my lover. my executioner.

I continued to ignore you
as you changed your mind and said:

"ACTUALLY. Go ahead! I want to crush you.
I want to make you so miserable you can't
 even move. Write about that."

And now that I am writing (about that)
I want to know.

How do you feel?

Do you feel proud?
Do you feel immortal?
...or do you just feel like an asshole?

Quick Question, Though:

Is it abuse...
if he had too much to drink?
if he's clearly spiraling? If he's young?
if he can't remember what he said?
if he can't remember what he did?
if he can't reach you as you push your weight
against the door?

Is it abuse...
if he hits himself in the face repeatedly
instead of hitting you?
(he didn't hit you, so it isn't, right?)

Is it abuse...
if he's nicer to you the next day
than he's ever been before?
if he gives you flowers with a written explanation?
(I have so many of those written explanations)

if he promises to change, if he apologizes?
if he has an undiagnosed bipolar disorder like your
therapist says?

...or maybe undiagnosed manic depressive?

I don't know, I'm not a doctor.

Is it abuse...
if his friends avoid your eyes
when you try to tell them
he's not as cool and funny
as they think he is?

Is it abuse...
if he says he loves you
and wants to marry you?

Is it abuse...
if you sort of forgive him?

Blank Page

I want to not think about you
the way you don't think about me.

I want things to remind you of me
but I don't want things to remind me of you.

I want you never to forget me
as I am trying to forget you.

*

(I would like to eternal sunshine
of the spotless mind you.)

Blue Eyeliner

They sell that blue eyeliner you like
so much at the sex shop on Belmont.

It felt strange marveling over all
the different colors while in the company
of flavored lube and edible panties.

I eavesdropped on the store employee
confidently weighing in on the differences
between waterproof vibrators and rechargeable bat-
teries as I found our favorite shade
of electric blue.

When people ask how we became friends,
I say I stalked you years ago at a beauty salon
(a more appropriate place to buy makeup).

And I'm totally okay with that cause it's hard
to find a friend like you, impossible, maybe,

and I love you...

even though you're so
goddamned gorgeous.

The Story About How You Changed My Life

For most of my 20s, I hated the name Holly.
Or rather...I hated the idea of her.

I didn't even know there was a Holly to dislike and that he was once married to one until about a month after we had begun dating. He was much older than me, 36 to my 22, and one of the few people to make a substantial impact on my life.

The night my friend introduced me to David at a bar in Ukrainian Village, I was wearing a pink turtleneck (it was 2005-ish) and had very blonde hair and he had on a striped collared t-shirt with a haircut that swept to the side.

(I used to remember the outfit of every man I met, his shirt, his shoes, his hair. I used to remember the very first thing he said to me. Now I can't remember anything at all.)

As I shook David's hand, my friend whispered in my ear, *he's old, like really old.*

I wasn't instantly attracted to David. In fact, I thought he was short and, as my friend said, too old.

He wasn't even on my radar as someone to date even though, later on, he would change my life in ways I never thought possible. He would be my champion.

At first, there were qualities of his that charmed their

way in. He was an editor of a free music magazine and at the time, I had wanted to start my own magazine, an endeavor I pursued with delusional enthusiasm. I couldn't fathom that anyone would publish me so I decided to publish myself.

Soon after that night we met, David asked to read some of my writing. I think he was really surprised to find he liked the way I wrote. I think most people are. I like that, when the bar is low. In return, he sent me articles he had written mostly about bands and politics, and I found out he was a damn good writer too (and after we broke up, a damn good vicious writer).

We hung out several times as friends. What I didn't realize was that maybe these hang outs were actually dates. I have absolutely no idea to this day whether or not I am on a date. It also hadn't occurred to me that I was someone David might be interested in. He was so clean cut, intelligent, well balanced and sane. At the time, I was clean up on aisle three, a huge mess. But I think maybe that was part of my appeal for him.

(I can already envision him scoffing at that last sentence as he reads this.)

On Valentine's Day, David took me to a sold out concert at the Metro for a band that I pretended to like. He spent most of the show on his blackberry, typing to someone. I stood around like an idiot trying to ignore his constant texting.

He said he was talking to a friend in Barcelona and he was, if anything, completely disinterested in the concert and me.

After the show, I lied and said I had to go to a funeral early the next day because I wasn't sure what else we could possibly do for the rest of the night. For what it's worth, there really was a funeral in my family, I can't recall whose, but I had no intention of going to it.

When he drove me home and parked in front of my studio apartment, I realized he was going to try to kiss me. There's something about a parked car at the end of the night that screams, kiss or no kiss, even with people you feel completely platonic with.

He didn't disappoint. When we went to hug goodnight, he leaned in to kiss me and I turned my entire head, knocking my nose into the shoulder of his leather jacket. His lips landed somewhere in a mess of my hair.

As I flew out of his car in a panic, I realized that I might actually like him.

*

When I finally decided I wanted to kiss David, I spent most of the evening playfully texting him from my apartment, hinting for him to invite me over. By around 2AM, he finally took the bait, saying he wished there was somehow I could see some movie he was telling me about but it was only at his place. This was back when people still bought and rented movies. I hopped in a cab immediately and was at his doorstep in 10 minutes.

I was shocked to find out that he lived in a big house all by himself. Nobody I knew lived in a house or lived alone, not when you're 22 and all your friends are poor.

Maybe this should have been my first clue about Holly.

When he invited me inside, I behaved in what can only be considered as strange and confusing (he would probably tell you that those 2 words describe how I behaved the entire time we dated).

Basically, I sat on the opposite side of his couch from him and barely spoke. He put on the movie and we sat in the dark, completely silent. It was so quiet that I had to be careful with how loudly I swallowed my own saliva and became very self-conscious of that.

After an agonizing hour of silence, he leaned all the way across the couch, put an arm around my waist and kissed my cheek. Then he said, "I'm sorry."

As in *I'm sorry for kissing you.*

Even though this was part of my plan, it took about 30 seconds for me to finally snap out of it and kiss him back. It was the kind of kiss that lasted until the sun rose. We didn't have sex, which I applauded myself for, but I know we both wanted to.

*

Our next "real" date after the kiss, David invited me to a BBQ to meet all his friends. Most of them were musicians in "cool" Chicago bands. I didn't know a single person there and they were all much older than me. I felt extremely intimidated by everyone and started to shut down. Sometimes, out of nowhere, I can become excruciatingly shy. It's been a problem my entire life. So, other than saying hello to everyone when I was first introduced to them, I didn't say a word at the BBQ. I'm serious, not a single word.

I sat in a chair on a porch and listened to everyone talk and joke and willed myself to be as small as possible. Back then, you couldn't just stare at your cell phone whenever you felt uncomfortable, you had to sit in that discomfort, actually experience it.

In that moment, I had become the least interesting person in the world. I had no original thoughts; my brain was empty. The only thought I had was *get me out of here.*

Nobody asked me anything either, as if they thought I might implode at the idea of being social. I became so stuck in my silence and felt so foolish, that I had to leave. I left without saying goodbye to anyone, a common move for someone with severe social anxiety. I caught a bus and cried in embarrassment the entire ride home. Nothing makes you more human than crying alone on public transportation. People are so polite and good at ignoring crying strangers. I thought to myself: I'm the kind of girl you can't take to a BBQ, who you can't introduce to your friends.

He was never going to talk to me again. I blew it.

But David was patient with me. I think it's because he was an older man, an actual adult and from a different generation.

(Right now I'm realizing that most men I've met and will meet will never give me that sort of chance again. They will dismiss me after one or two dates without much thought, without any patience. They won't see the value in finding out who I am. And I'm learning not to take it personally. Nobody has the attention span for love anymore.)

After my mute performance with David and his friends, he ended up calling me back and we began dating. When we laughed about it later, all he said was after the BBQ he was completely puzzled and thought to himself:

what am I going to do with this girl?

I don't think he ever figured out the answer to that question.

*

Thinking back to the first time David and I slept together, I remember that he had fucked me like a real man. I felt as if everyone before him didn't know the meaning of fucking. I was quite impressed by it, actually.

I didn't cum but I almost could have.

The morning after our first fuck (he will read this and tell me that I still don't know how to use curse words in my writing, *stop using curse words in your writing*), there was a light rain and he grabbed a pink umbrella and we walked together to the Ukrainian grocery store down the street.

I remember feeling awestruck not only by our sex the night before but by the fact that he could confidently carry around a pink umbrella and not give two shits.

Now, I realize, that pink umbrella must have been Holly's.

*

It was around week 5 of us dating that I found out about her. We were at one of those gritty 4AM bars in Chicago and I said to him (looking back now, I cringe as this scene plays in my head),

I asked, "How on earth is it possible that you're 36 and not married? You're, like, the perfect guy."

I went on to list all of his great qualities. He had a

a good job. He was well-read. He introduced me to new music. He could write. He was up to date with current events. He could cook. He was easy going. I actually learned new things from him.

As I rambled on, David set down his drink and blinked a few times.

Then he carefully said, "I thought you knew this already...I used to be married."

My heart sank and then pounded loudly in my ears. WHAT?? All the chaos around us, drunk people, loud music, spilled drinks, dimmed lights, it made me dizzy and there was that feeling again...Fight or Flight. I had to leave. I practically ran out of the bar.

Remember, I was 22. I had never dated someone who *used* to be married. My parents, your parents used to be married, not the guy I was sleeping with. I hadn't really had a serious boyfriend at this point and David had already gotten down on one knee for someone else. Had a wedding, a honeymoon, dreams and plans. He had already had a whole life with her, a life that for whatever reason ended.

David followed me outside, breathless and said, "I'm sorry. I just assumed you knew."

I am not sure how I would have known if he hadn't told me but I suddenly pretended like I was totally okay with this new information. After all, we had only known each other a few weeks and I was still in the playing it cool phase.

I worry that I've tried to play it cool my whole life and it's never gotten me anywhere but nowhere.

I signaled for a cab and he asked, rather desperately, if he could join me. We both got in. He gave the cab driver the address to his house, a house I had once been so impressed by, and said, "let me explain."

Instead, I put my hand on his thigh and kissed him roughly. I didn't want him to explain. I didn't want to know anything or I was sure I would die. I was probably already in love with him at that point.

I kissed him hard the whole cab ride home, my hand on his belt buckle, my finger slipping just a bit into the top of his waistband so that he couldn't think about anything else.

My kiss said, *I am totally okay with this, let's move on.*

But my brain was on fire.

*

Shit. I just realized this is a common pattern of mine. Instead of having a mature, adult conversation when I'm upset with someone I'm dating, I brush it off and have sex with them instead. Or I brush it off and never speak of it (or to them) again.

This can't be healthy for anyone, probably.

*

After that night, "Holly" clues began to pop up completely uninvited, although they must have always been there. His house with the creaky wooden staircase and extra, empty rooms upstairs suddenly felt so heavy and sad to me. I imagined him and Holly buying that house together, careful to find a place with a backyard and extra rooms for their future children.

I imagined her having her own collection of recipes. I imagined them watching movies where he first kissed me. Planting flowers around the house. Picking out baby names. I felt sad for him and sad for her and sad for myself. I knew that I could never be the kind of woman I had decided Holly was. I could never promise a man that we would have one, two children. That we needed a backyard. That we save up for a house. I would never suggest we paint those dining room halls dark red.

(Holly must have, right?)

Holly,
Holly,
Holly.
She had gotten there first.

Where was she now?

The first real clue I found was the catalogs that piled up on his covered front porch. We liked to sit there sometimes at night. His street was so quiet you could hear crickets and other insects and it didn't feel at all like you lived in a city.

But there, tucked along with his mail were various catalogs. Pottery Barn, Crate & Barrel, Nordstrom, J. Crew, Anthropologie.

These catalogs were who told me her name. There it was, attached to his own last name, in some sort of menacing nod toward me. They also told me that Holly had her shit together. She was the kind of woman who wore a cashmere cardigan while cooking dinner with her contemporary non-stick 12 piece cookware set. And under that cashmere sweater, was a $75 bra that matched a $45 pair of panties that you had to hand wash and Holly didn't throw them in the washer anyway.

Holly must be the kind of woman whose coffee cups match her bowls match her dinner plates match her side plates match her silverware. Holly had the lids to all her Tupperware, no matter what size it was. Holly had a flat stomach and didn't need antidepressants.

In case you didn't catch on, Holly was just a fruition of all my shortcomings and insecurities as a 22 year old. I wish that 22 year old knew how smart and talented and alive she actually was instead of wasting so much time hating herself.

When David saw me notice the catalogs, even in the dark, he pushed all the mail together into one neat pile and said, "I don't know how to get them to stop coming. Every month, they come." So the catalogs were taunting him too.

The second real clue was this time we were in his basement. It had flooded and he needed to clear out some books. He handed me a copy of *Tropic of Cancer* and I opened it curiously. In the margins of many pages of the book, there was this delicate, dainty handwriting. Notes on whatever passage she had just read. I shuddered to myself at the thought of her loving authors like Henry Miller.

That means she might actually be smart, she might actually be interesting, even worse...she might be a writer. Then I decided Holly must actually be a nurse, she must be a kindergarten teacher, she must be an advertising executive, she must be the vice president. Those were the kinds of women a man like David would marry.

*

A few nights later, I sat at a bar and asked our mutual friend who was working there if he had known about the elusive Holly.

He wiped the counter, shook his head and said:

"OHH yeah, that was REALLY fucked up."

I nodded in agreement but never asked him to elaborate on his comment.

*

Eventually, Holly faded from the picture. I never asked David about her and he never volunteered any information. I now know that every relationship will have a Holly. And I will be the Holly in someone else's relationship. And we have to be okay with that.

David and I found common ground in the music industry. We both wanted to help our favorite musicians with booking, with management, with PR. We wanted to be their champions and we became a dream team power couple for one musician in particular.

What I didn't know was that I needed my own champion. And after two years of dating, David became mine.

*

Some days, a morning
is just a morning.

Some days a morning
can change your life.

*

The morning that changed my life was in the spring at David's house. I always woke up much later than him because I fell asleep much later. He was already downstairs, he had already made coffee, watered his garden, answered emails, he was such an adult. I sleepily sat down next to him on the couch and he pulled out his phone.

On his phone was an image of a painting, it was blue with an old fashioned bicycle, the kind you might see at a circus with one massive wheel in the front.

The image was nostalgic and beautiful. I recognized the style; it was clearly made by my friend and artist Shawn.

I said, "What is this? A new painting? A new band poster?"

He said, "No, this is the cover for your book."

I looked at the image confused, "What do you mean my book?"

He said, "YOUR BOOK," and pulled out of his bag a massive manuscript with a giant clip holding it together. He handed it to me. The first page said *Piano Rats*. I looked at him in confusion. I hadn't written a book.

He smiled.

"I took all of your stories you sent me and all the stories on your blogs and I put the best ones together into a manuscript. They are formatted easily so all you need to do is print it. This is YOUR book and it's good! It's really good. I'm going to make sure you go through with this."

I was still in shock as I took the manuscript from his hands and started flipping through it. There was even an index for each story. He must've been working on this for months. There were stories I had written years ago and stories written weeks ago.
Many of them were sad. Some were sexy, about men who weren't him. They were too honest and that scared me.

The title *Piano Rats* was brilliant, perfect. I can't ever take credit for that. I felt a strange rush come from the pages, a strange rush from him. It was the most powerful, beautiful thing anyone had ever done for me.

I began to cry. I had always wanted to write a book but I had waited for the characters and arcs and plots and storylines that never arrived. He saw past that. He saw the value of what I had been writing for myself and made a home for it.

He gave me courage to be myself. I didn't just cry, I wept. Nobody had ever done anything like that for me before. Nobody has done anything like that for me since.

*

When I tell him now that I have a story about him in my new book, he is less than enthusiastic. He says, "oh great." Though he's used to this.

Even though we haven't seen each other in years. Even though he's married to the girl he met after me.

(By the way, they are all married to the girl after me.)

David said, "I know you and I know your writing. And I know myself and our relationship. If I come off bad, I'm okay with it."

"No, no," I said, "you don't understand. This is the story about how you changed my life."

He replied with, "Oh, I thought it was gonna be about coke and sex and bad haircuts."

*

At first, *Piano Rats* brought us closer. That summer, we edited it excitedly together on my yellow couch, splitting the manuscript into a pile of good stories and bad stories. He was a saint for editing stories I had written about other men, the men before him.

I finally felt like I had someone who really understood me. It's a hard feeling to hold onto when you find it. I would give anything to experience that feeling with another person again. Someone who believes in you. Someone who believes in your art.

The book wasn't enough to save our relationship, though. I don't know what it was but there was some sort of electrical switch in my heart that flipped from ON to OFF. He didn't do anything wrong. Nothing had changed. If anything, something magical had happened: I had a book now.

But still, there is no other way to describe it. Just suddenly, I didn't want to be with him anymore and he didn't want to be with me if I didn't want to be with him.

I fell out of love, which sounds simple but is incredibly difficult to make sense of because for almost an entire year after, I was paralyzed with sadness over him. And I lost my mind when he found someone after me, his new Holly.

Like most relationships, David and I had to untangle our lives together. It didn't end well but it wasn't a relationship I regret. He is still managing the musician I had encouraged him to work with years before. I'm still writing books.

We had altered the course of each other's lives in positive ways, which is a beautiful, nearly impossible love to find in another person and I'm so grateful to have experienced that.

(so, thank you for changing my life.)

24th & Mission

I learned more than I ever wanted to know about Syphilis because of Peter. Peter wasn't my lover. He played the tin whistle at the 24th and Mission Bart station in San Francisco.

I know his name because we took turns. Took turns "busking" for money, that is.

The first time I saw him, he reminded me of a scarecrow, dangly arms and legs, rolled up jeans and mismatched socks. I think he might have been about 60 or so years old.

He caught eyes with me and said, "Found this flute in the grass at the park...who knew I could already play it?"

Every time a crowd rolled past him after a train emptied out, he'd clear his throat and shout, "This is Tchaikovsky's Serenade in D Minor," and then he'd blow into that whistle so hard he nearly fell over, dizzy.

In the month that I've been watching (and waiting my turn), Peter's never once played a recognizable melody and I knew that he had no idea who Tchaikovsky really was and I think that was why I liked him so much.

It's so boring and exhausting trying to impress people all the time.

Whenever he finished playing, he'd either do a little tap dance and smile in a way that revealed his missing front tooth or shake his cup sadly and complain about how cheap people are.

Then he'd respectfully nod at me.
"The floor is yours, Miss."

And I'd unpack my violin to play.

Peter had another act too.

Aside from the tin whistle, he had acquired at the free health clinic on Haight Street a giant pamphlet with all the trials and tribulations of Syphilis. Some days, usually when he forgot his tin whistle, he'd just stand as tall as he could, making wide gestures with those gangly arms and recite the statistics of the dreaded disease.

Peter would often state, "SYPHILIS IS BACK."

This was his favorite line: "Syphilis can occur on the external genitals, vagina, anus, rectum, lips and mouth."

He would read that as if it were a hidden gem in a Joan Didion essay.

When he was done, he'd carefully fold up the pamphlet and tuck it in his denim jacket pocket and say to me, "This is the only book I have. Read it front to back many times."

On Peter's Syphilis act days, he made very little money. In fact, he generally accumulated candy wrappers, discarded tissues and dirty looks in his cup instead.

He'd look inside and sorely say, "Just educating the people, Miss, but they don't appreciate it. Your turn now, play us a good one."

He never once asked me what I was doing down there, at 19 years old with my violin. He never acted as if I didn't belong and I was grateful.

Despite growing up with years of violin lessons, like Peter, my repertoire for the train station was slim. I had forgotten all the concertos Mr. Sokolov had forced me to memorize and was left with only three melodies that I could play by memory.

They were the most desperately lonely violin pieces I had ever heard and played. A sad Jewish hymn (Kaddish). An even sadder traditional Irish ballad. And some Norwegian Dances by Grieg that were un-recognizable to most people. I certainly wasn't here to please the crowds but it seemed to work in my favor.

I usually leaned against the brick wall and only be-gan to play when a wave of people were leaving the train. It would be dead silent and then for about two full minutes, people flew past me without much thought, pausing just enough to toss $1 or $5 into my violin case.

The first day I busked, after 45 minutes, I made $60 and I knew it was worth the embarrassment of begging for money. For the first time in weeks, I could buy groceries. I traded in my packets of Kool-Aid for real juice and stocked up on peanut butter and jelly. I began to do it whenever I needed to buy food.

One particularly successful afternoon, I didn't realize Peter was behind me, intently watching me count my money. When I finished, he did his little tap dance and let out a loud whistle. "Wow. I've only made $15 at the most playing down here. Must be because you're a young lady."

After Peter discovered our difference in busking wages, he would always let me play first. Then he'd wait for me to pack up and we'd count my earnings together and I'd give him half. It didn't matter how different our lives were, him in the halfway house and me with my apartment full of drug addict artists. We were both here for the same reason so we shared a mutual respect (or sympathy) for one another.

And so we became friends of sorts. I learned little bits and pieces about his life and volunteered little information about myself. I learned that Peter had never fought in a war but his brother did. "He lost his right arm to gangrene and got so depressed he shot himself left-handed." Peter had a wife once who was a beautiful florist but she left him for another woman. He even had a son he lost touch with living somewhere in New Mexico.

He told me these things like they were facts in the Syphilis pamphlet rather than landmark events in his life.

He also told me that before he met me, he had never really heard the violin and he would like to learn to play.

One particular day, I showed up at the train station with my violin to find Peter already there and in a crazy state. He was pacing and holding the Syphilis pamphlet and had a wild look in his eyes, shouting about government conspiracies and God.

He was making quite a scene and people rushed by in alarm and fear. What was worse, was some people were stopping to laugh at him.

I stood back and my heart sank with the realization that Peter had a very real illness and a diminishing sense of reality. He was proving that his stay at the halfway house and his bouts of homelessness and garbage picking were not just a rough patch he was wrestling through, this was the hand he was dealt.

Finally, he was shouting so loud and banging the Syphilis pamphlet so hard against the brick wall that I knew I had to stop him.

I reached into my violin case and pulled out my copy of Kurt Vonnegut's *Slaughterhouse-Five* and went up to him.

"Peter...PETER, can you be quiet for a minute? I need your help. Please?"

He stopped yelling for a second and looked at me with tears all caught up in his wrinkled cheeks. I could tell for a minute he didn't recognize me.

"What? What do you need?" He said it almost accusingly.

I said I wanted to trade books. I was tired of my book and I really wanted his book instead. I motioned to the pamphlet in his hand.

"Please?"

He looked down at my book, his eyes widened in wonder. He let out a grin with that one tooth poking out and seemed visibly calmer. "Sure, anything for Miss Violinist over here."

And we sealed the deal. He gave me the now very dirty and tattered educational Syphilis pamphlet, and I gave him my very dirty and tattered copy of *Slaughterhouse-Five*.

We shook hands and Peter did a little tap dance and bounced away, shouting about his new book that he was waving in the air.

As I unpacked my violin and got ready to play, I knew that I'd never see him again and as a nod from the universe, I only made $10 that day.

I never busked again after that and I never saw Peter either but I have a feeling that he's reading Vonnegut out loud at another train station somewhere, anywhere in America,

maybe even New Mexico.

Things That People Do in the Winter

Forever goodbyes always end with the words *good luck.*

You were pacing quietly on the sidewalk outside of my place and I could feel the heaviness between us all the way from the top of the stairs. I couldn't see the expression on your face as I walked down because I wasn't wearing my glasses but I had an idea of what it might be. I knew it well; you wore it all summer.

When I finally reached you, we forgot how to talk like people who have known each other for years. We forgot how to talk at all and finally you just said,

"I miss you."

A thousand years passed before I said, "I miss you too." But it came out high, hollow and insincere. The truth was I didn't know how to miss you. I missed the person I thought you were but you had become someone I didn't know.

Before you landed on that sidewalk, I had checked my makeup, changed my shirt, ran a hand through my hair. I knew it didn't matter, you had seen me at my worst, but it seemed important that I looked put together even if you had torn me apart.

It's strange how a feeling for someone can change from immeasurable excitement to thick dread in a matter of months. Thick. Dread.

You asked for a hug even though I hate hugging you because of the vast difference of how you seem to have SO MUCH LOVE and I seem to be hung up to dry. This hug was no different, I was stiff and cautious.

You said you were sad. I said I was sad too.

Then, on this unseasonably warm October night, I handed you the keys to my former apartment and you handed me $450 in an envelope with my name on it. We've exchanged many letters over the years and I recognized the writing and knew it would be the last one from you.

There was a silence before you said, "Maybe we can get coffee sometime or do those things that people do in the winter, whatever they are."

I simply answered "no" and it looked for a minute like you might cry so I turned away. I wanted to hurt you the way you hurt me.

No apologies were offered. No peace treaty. No explanation. No forgiveness. We had dug ourselves too deep for that. We had dug a grave.

Then we did the thing that finalizes the end to any friendship, relationship, emotional connection, whatever. We very awkwardly and insincerely wished each other good luck.

I said it first, as you were already walking away.
"Hey...Good luck."

"Yeah, good luck to you too."
And you were gone.

I've been sad, you had said.

You once were the only person who truly understood my sadness (and I the only one who understood yours) and now we were the cause of it.

That was the last time we ever saw each other.

Just Read

I'm holding my new book in his new apartment in Bucktown. I know he's been waiting to read it. I had talked about it so much at this point but fear and lack of money had kept me from printing it until now.

He had just moved to Chicago unexpectedly from a small town in Wisconsin. We had been dating long distance for about a year but not too seriously, I thought.

He was from the kind of town where he woke up at 5AM and crushed ice and delivered it to all the local bars and restaurants and houses. A job that was 100 years old and the horse carriage once used for deliveries was still in front of the icehouse to prove it.

He once showed me a blurry, discolored polaroid of two young girls bundled up in a snowy parking lot and said, "This is the only photograph I have of my sisters." I wondered about those sisters occasionally.

I turn down his record player and say, "You can't have this book, you know. This is the only one I have."

"Okay." He never says anything mean to me ever. His kindness is unexpected and welcome. His eyes, soft. He has muscles that my friends jokingly say are from "working on the farm" and his good looks are almost as painful as his shyness.

He's read most of my stories in the book anyway because I had sent them to him via letters and emails. Still, he lies down on the bed and excitedly asks me to read.

I lie next to him on my stomach and prop myself up on my elbows nervously. I shift through some pages of my book and begin to blush at certain poems. I am suddenly ashamed of my own art, of my own thoughts, of how bold I sometimes am.

"I can't read you these. Most of these are about old lovers. Sex. Break ups. Some of these are so sad."

He says patiently, "Just read. I like when you do."

Oftentimes that winter, we stayed in bed and read to each other. It was kind of like foreplay for people who love Kundera and Melville. We would do it shyly at first and then with more confidence. He would pull out his typewriter and we'd type stories on the spot, switching places, finishing each other's sentences.

He was a beautiful writer and before he had moved, he filled my mailbox with many long letters and type-written stories. It's a rare thing these days, to have someone write letters to you.

I rummaged through my new book and began to read, avoiding his eyes completely.

I read my favorite one, the first page, a safe choice.

And then I read another and another and another. He listened quietly, without judgement or comment but when I was done, I saw his face had changed, his eyes had changed.

I closed the book for a moment and said, "You're falling in love with me right now, aren't you?"

I've never said that to anyone before but I know he liked it. He didn't deny it.

Love becomes so easy when neither person is denying it, when we lean into it instead of away.

On paper, he was what I had been always looking for. An intelligent guy who loved books and old records and typewriters and handwritten letters and kissing all night and drinking tea instead of whiskey. Someone who was genuine and never cocky. He said what he meant and actually meant it. He wasn't running around searching for other people, it was as if he had been searching only for me. Plato's idea of a soul mate.

"Don't worry," I said, closing the book. "You'll be in the next one."

(Here you are, this one's for you.

And I'm so sorry, by the way, for how it all ended.

I never got to tell you that so I'm telling you now.)

It Ends with a Misleading Kiss

Tonight you will kiss a girl who isn't sure if she is pretty. You will try and show her the stars but they are just soup can lids with jagged edges. She will reach out to touch one and slice her finger. When she begins to bleed you will slip away because suddenly she is real and real isn't what you're looking for.

You will crawl 2000 miles across the desert until you find a shiny, black grand piano. The girl who isn't sure if she is pretty will try and follow but gets lost somewhere in Reno.

Inside the grand piano you will find 17 dead mockingbirds. Like a god, you will press upon their shallow chests and bring them back to life because you are lonely. They will come to in a flash of color and are anything but friendly, so they fly away.

Alone in the desert, you will realize you are nothing but a collection of reactions, your most recent reaction is to a now four day old kiss that you wish to recapture. You will spend light years working your way back to the girl who isn't sure if she is pretty.

After such a long journey, you will find her: she is fast asleep inside the moment right before you first touched her shoulder.

She is a quiet sleeper and you will touch her once again to activate a slow smile. When she finally opens her eyes, you will have to look away because you see inside them a prayer that hasn't been recited in 1700 years.

The prayer is a meditation on moments so slight that it is easy to miss them.

She will say, "There is something I wanted to tell you but I can't remember what it is."

And you will wait and wait for her to remember but she never does because all of this began (and ended)

with
a
misleading kiss.*

Franki Elliot is the critically-acclaimed author of *Piano Rats* and *Kiss As Many Women As You Can*. Her work has been nationally recognized by *Paper Magazine, The Paris Review, VICE, Amy Poehler Smart Girls, Chicago Tribune, LA Weekly, Time Out*, etc. Her books are complimented with stunning artwork by Shawn Stucky, a red/green color-blind artist. This is her third book and she currently lives in Los Angeles.